CW00501195

CLATTER OF CLOGS

A collection of mining memories at
the end of an era.

by

COLIN GIBBS

Clatter of Clogs
© 2006 Colin Gibbs
© 2006 Typesetting and layout Bridge Books
This second edition published in Wales
by
BRIDGE BOOKS
61 Park Avenue
Wrexham
LL12 7AW
on behalf of the author

ISBN 1-84494-026-8

1st Edition published 1990
Reprinted 1991

**Winner of the Certificate of Merit in the Clwyd Voluntary Service Council's
prestigeous Local Endeavour Competition 1990, in recognition of its
contribution to the preservation of community life.**

CIP Data for this book is available
from the British Library

Cover illustration: An injured man, Harry Pierce, is brought out
from the Hafod after a roof fall. [*Liverpool Daily Post & Echo*]

Printed and bound by
Cromwell Press Ltd
Trowbridge

This book is dedicated to all those who have struggled to earn a living in coal-mining and as a memorial to those who sacrificed their lives in the attempt.

The title, *Clatter of Clogs*, has been taken from a conversation with a local miner:

> 'I remember when I was a boy, all you could hear at 5 a.m. was the clatter of clogs. People going to work would rely on the clogs to wake them up. It was more reliable than an alarm clock.'
>
> Colin Reese

Contents

Bersham Colliery.

Prologue

Hafod miner, Manager of Bersham Colliery and former
Member of Parliament and Member of the
European Parliament

Coal mining has always been an intensely human industry. Warm comradeship has transcended the discomfort and dangers. Not for us the boredom of the factory; the assembly line, the solitude of the farmer in his 'rough acreage fenced by the rain'; the frustration of the teacher at the blackboard, or even the anguish of the clergyman writing:

> *on men's hearts and in the minds of young children sublime words too often forgotten …*

We had humour instead. Simple, droll, sometimes ironic, never cruel and always heartfelt. We laughed with gusto in good times and bad.

Looking back, I sometimes think we were blessed more than we realised with this gift of the heart. It made us a fraternity, able to see things in perspective, and proud to belong to a true brotherhood.

I congratulate the vicar and the parishioners of Penycae on deciding to produce this book. The vicar will be better aware than most people that speakers at wedding receptions, when referring to a couple beginning their married life, often use the cliché about the patter of tiny feet. The 'Clatter of Clogs' is no cliché. It is an imaginative commemoration of an industry which dominated this part of the world for nearly two centuries, and of the men who worked in it and sometimes died in it.

I am privileged to write this prologue. I do so conscious of what I owe to a great industry and to the great men who worked in it. I commend Clatter of Clogs to you all.

TED MCKAY

Former North Wales Miners' Agent

Although the pit wheels have long since stopped turning, it is a fact that wherever miners meet to have a chat, they will be still hewing the coal of long ago, recalling names, places and incidents from their days underground.

But, if asked what they miss most about the pit, invariably they will say 'the lads', adding that no-one could have worked with finer men. 'We were all our brother's keeper down there.' They will also tell you that in the most difficult situations underground someone would always say something to break the tension.

Equally, they would tell you, even though they would not have changed their life, they would not want any one else to work in those conditions or to have those underground experiences. Yet it is those conditions and experiences that gave rise to the camaraderie and unique character that typifies all those who have worked below the surface, wherever it might be.

After 500 years, mining in North Wales has gone, and with it a distinct way of life that was both hard and humourous, but also very caring. It is hoped that all who read this book will get a fleeting glimpse and catch the voices of the miners of North Wales.

I am but one of very many who are grateful to Colin Gibbs for his interest and sympathetic study of the miners' daily toil which puts an essential 'last personal word' into the collection of our social history.

August 2006

Foreword

The echoes of laughter, the joy of singing, the mirth of storytelling, the reality of companionship at home, in work, or in the church and chapel environment. Many of these experiences are chronicled in this very useful book. They come to life once again as we recall memories of the past. Why not? For they are part of our human experiences which have in turn fashioned our lives.

Ie, amheuthun felly yw cael ailbrofi cofiant gorffennol Penycae yn y gyfrol hon. Bydded bendith ar eich mwynhad ohoni.

May you receive a blessing in your reading of this hook.

> Alwyn St Asaph
> Bishop of St Asaph
> Archbishop of Wales

Esgobty, St Asaph

Acknowledgements

The first discovery I made about miners is that despite the harshness of the working conditions they endure and the history of betrayal that stalks the darkest corridors of their relationship with the 'bosses', they remain a warm and jolly community of mates with just a hint of shyness when asked to speak about their hard life underground. It is an existence that seems to be supported on twin pillars of loyalty and laughter, and in this collection of memories both these characteristics are evident.

I have tried to let the authentic voice of the miners come through in the telling of these tales, without too much editing. I hope in this way I have been able to retain the freshness of the incident and some of the local flavour and dialect. I make no apology for the lack of explanation of place names. This is a local book for local people who know the places and many of the tale-tellers. I hope though, that readers further afield will still be able to relish the moment with us. No offence is intended by the choices I have made, and no claim is made about technical accuracy either. The stories are very much as they have been told to me.

This collection comes largely from the Rhos and Penycae area and the pit that has supported these communities most is The Hafod. It is to the men of The Hafod and their families, as well as those of other pits who spoke with me. that my debt of gratitude is owed the most.

But I must thank particular miners from my own parish: Emlyn Davies, Vic Evans, Colin Reese, Bill (Sophie) Jones,

Neville Davies, Eric Jones and Jackie Read as well as Tom Ellis and Ted McKay for their encouragement and patient guidance. I acknowledge also the help of Ysgol Grango for loan of taping equipment; Gillian Griffiths for her help in typing and retyping many pages of manuscript; John Williams for his help in Welsh translation; Jenny, my wife, the great 'enthusiast'; and Spike Hill, Head of Fulcrum Graphics London — an old friend — for his design expertise with the production of the first edition.

This page would not be complete without my thanks to everyone who contributed towards the success of the *Clatter of Clogs* commemorative service for local pits held in the parish church in April 1989. It was the largest congregation the church has ever seen.

I hope you find as much enjoyment in these memories as I have discovered in researching them and that others consider them to be a fit companion for the 'last lump' mined at The Hafod and now residing in a place of honour at the Hafod Miners Club.

At the end of an era, all that remains to be said to the men and their families is 'Thank You'.

C.H.G.
2006

The profit from the first edition was given to the Miners' Convalescent Home in Blackpool.
L–R: Ted McKay, Jackie Read, Author, three NUM officials, Vic Evans, Emlyn Davies.

Echoing Laughter

The first lesson learned by an apprentice is that miners everywhere have a great sense of fun. Jokes of all kinds have been pulled; some worked into a gigantic leg pull involving many men, but most often the simple exchange of that swift retort so typical of miners. Nearly everyone speaking in this book have their own particular favourite and here are some of those given to me.

A retired miner still has vivid recollection of his first day down the pit as a 14-year old boy. After describing a ³⁄₄ mile trip down in the cage and being left by himself he was taken to an area known as the Flats.

He took me down after to what we called the flats, where the horses were. Now there were about six horses there and different young men working with the horses. When I got in I had quite a sensation, to be honest, because these horses some of them were very gentle and others were very wild and kicking. In this particular flat there was one horse, very nasty and he came down screaming, and I jumped out of his way into a trough full of water. That was my first day down the pit.

A well known tool in Hafod was a 'Jim Crow'. We used it to bend or straighten a rail and many a young lad coming down the pit has been sent for Jim Crow. He was always told to keep on walking to the next district because Jim Crow was down there. They never thought it was a tool. They always assumed it was a man.

The under manager shouted out 'Eh what's the matter down there? There's nothing moving.'
The answer echoed back 'It's Ken Mule. He's not going to work in the pit bottom. It's too cold.'

'What can we do then?' shouted the Under Manager.

'Well' came back the reply. 'Ken Mule would like a Donkey Jacket.'

Everyone wanted to know at 5:15 a.m. 'Where's the cat this morning.?' If it sat on the table in the cabin of Ben Pritchard the Under Manager, all was well. If not, we were in trouble for we knew the cat vanished only when Ben banged the table in a bad mood.

Before nationalisation we worked a three day week. The hooter would blow at 6 p.m. to tell men there was no work that day. Llew Ezekiel Phillips would shout to Mary his wife, 'Duw, Handel never composed sweeter music than that!'

There was an unwritten rule below ground that coal would be left 'down' ready for the next shift to start earning without having to cut coal. On one occasion this understanding was ignored. Before the next shift left they made their feelings known by chalking on the new unscarred face — 'Rock of ages left for me, I will do the same to Thee.'

An elderly miner was given the job of bringing up the latrine buckets from the pit bottom and emptying them.

Quite apart from the unpleasantness of this essential job, he was regularly ridiculed by a group of bricklayers who were engaged in alterations at the pit head. One day he realised he could not take any more of this cruel banter, so he devised his own plan to put a stop to it.

Next time he came up with his consignment of high smelling muck, sure enough the brickies began their insulting remarks. Instead of going to the regular place for disposing of the latrines the old miner headed straight for the cement mixing machines and proceeded to empty all the latrines into them. Turning proudly on his heel he tossed over his shoulder the remark: 'There you are lads, mix that lot up.' The stench was so overpowering that all the offices had to be evacuated and the management were furious. Needless to say the insults stopped abruptly.

Strength games play a big part in the mining humour. Two miners boasted within earshot of colleagues that they were stronger than the other, and it became clear that a trial of strength was likely. Miners love these moments and so it was decided that each would try to punch a hole in an old rotting barn door on the way home that night. Naturally on their journey home that evening they were pursued by an eager crowd of miners wanting to see who was the stronger, placing a bet or two, and hoping they would make fools of themselves. When the door was reached the first man squared up to it. The huge ham like fist went back in a great arc and then faster than the eye could follow swept forward and smashed with a sickening thud into the thickest part of the door which did not yield an inch. His fist bounced off the woodwork and obviously in great pain he thrust the injured hand into his pocket and turning on his heel, without a nod stalked away. Later it was revealed by his father that his fist was so badly damaged, swollen and bleeding that when he got home it had to be cut out of his trouser pocket. To add insult to injury the second miner declined the challenge altogether.

Jonathan asked us this day to put stonedust bags on his chest. He was lying down and these bags weighed 1 *cwt* each. He wanted to see how much he could lift up. Another time we tied him with lashing chains, but without him knowing we tied the chain together with shot-firing wire so that it would break easy. Everybody used to walk past him sideways for him to pass. Because his shoulders were so wide, or so he thought. I remember he had a job painting and fireproofing the timber wearing a very heavy plastic coat and we challenged him to walk out of the pit wearing this coat. And he marched out and the sweat was pouring out of him. Because he wanted to show how strong he was, you see. Travelling on the bus to Cefn, everybody would sit on one side and put Jonathan on the other to even up the bus and he believed it.

Then there was the man who thought he had the biggest chest in Hafod, and some of the boys measured him by some props on a junction by putting the tape around the props as well as his chest. When he saw the measurement it made his day and he really thought he had the largest chest.

There was one man and he was very strong, working on the loading point in Hafod. He was in charge of loading all the dirt and this particular night there were a lot of stones coming off. They used to come at a good rate if there were a lot of men on the ripping and a big stone came and went over the side of the tub onto the floor. So this fellow goes and gets this stone, and it was a big stone, but he could lift it quite easily and he was trying to break it on the railside. Well, another fellow working close by came to him and said: 'Listen' he said, 'You are lifting that stone higher than the tub. Don't try and break it, put it straight into the tub.' That hadn't occurred to him you see.

Miners developed their own code on the knockin wire to let others know the bosses were coming into the district. Of course Bob Ellis, Hafod Under-Manager, was well aware of these codes and one day old Eddie Bellis was there on the engine, and he knocked two fours on the signalling wire to let the men inside know that Bob was on his way in. Bob went back to him and said 'What's two fours Eddie?' Eddie replied 'Eight Mr. Ellis.'

There were two engine drivers in No. 1 — Eric Tunnah and Fred the Lad. Fred would sing all day long, always wide awake and Eric could sleep at the drop of a hat. When Bob Ellis used to walk up he would say: 'On one side the graveyard and on the other the Concert Hall!'

Bob Ellis was a deacon in the chapel and a very well respected man. More powerful in the colliery than the manager. He knew everybody and their family. When you first started and you had to see him, he would tell you more about your family than you ever

Miners at Colwyn Bay Eisteddfod, 1947. William Tunnah from the Hafod is standing last on the right. [Mrs E. Morris]

knew. 'Oh yes I'll put you with your uncle' he would say and I never knew I had an uncle until he told me.

Glyn Whitescarf was known for his drinking, and we used to challenge him to drink a gallon of water straight down before going down the pit. And he could do it. A yard of ale would have been nothing to him. Great character was Glyn.'

If ever there was an electrical breakdown and Bob Ellis was down the pit he would go on the phone and he used to say to the man on the switchboard: 'Would you please put me through to Butlin's Holiday Camp'. Cos that's what he thought of electricians. He thought they never worked'.

Spirits were high just before Christmas and pit bottom phones had not been installed long. This night, Christmas Eve it was, we decided to play a joke on the man in the cabin. He always used to answer the phone shouting:

17

'Who is it this time?' even if no one had called him before. So we decided we'd all ring him up. First one came on.

'Who is it this time?' he shouted. and the answer came back:

'It's Father Christmas.'

And we kept this up all night, everyone saying: 'This is Father Christmas.'

Anyhow later on that shift there was a fall and now we rang up for help, you see. But he got his own back:

'If you want help' he shouted, 'Get some of those bloody Father Christmases' to help you. There's plenty of them down there somewhere!'

There would be a rush for the first ride out known as the first rope. Chapel choir members would congregate together on the three deck cage. Other miners would crouch or sit in the two much smaller decks. So popular was this first cage up that only the very fit miners made it. Men would run headlong towards the pit bottom and some men would dive in on top of crouching miners just to be on it. Leaving districts early to ensure a place was common and this tale is typical of the quick wits of men from Hafod:

'Old Bill Prodger and some of us were going out this day, to catch the first rope, about 12.30 p.m. You weren't supposed to go out until one o'clock. And we were going through this airway door and Bill was leading, and who was coming in but Harry Gittings the manager.

Harry took one look at him and said: 'Bill where are you going now?'

'Back now I've seen you' Bill said.

Visitors coming to Hafod were brought to listen to the singing as the cage came up on the first rope. The men wanted to get up first to have the first bath you see. Nobody wanted to have to queue for a shower, so they tried to get on the first rope.

I worked with a man by the name of Dick Margate. A very strong man. When we used to walk out, working nights, we came out through the old return. He was a big eater. Everything he done was half strained you know. I'm not saying he had no brains, but he always did something the hardest way and we had another old man, a chap by the name of Bryn Mair and Dick used to say to Bryn:

'What you got for breakfast this morning Mair?'

'Rice Crispies and a light boiled egg, what have you got Dick?'

'Half a bucket of lob scouse!'

Bill Thomas, Chief Fitter, was in a bad mood that morning in the pit bottom cabin before we left. And we gotta take a horse in with us to haul some heavy parts up a supply road. Bill was still in a mood and ready to snap your head off. It was Arthur Jones, Gladys Jones brother, who fetched the horse and was by the cabin, with Bill still in a bad mood. So Arthur lifted Rover's top and bottom jaw:

'Bill' he said, 'Look at Rover laughing at us.'

The way he did it made us all roar with laughter. Everybody in the cabin was laughing and Bill Thomas too.

'Well' he said, 'That's made my day that 'as. I've never seen a horse laughing before!'

And his mood changed just like that. We were all laughing going in.

The *Iron Horse* to Bill Thomas wasn't just a song. He believed that if you sang it the machinery went better. And he'd tell them off for laughing and for not singing it properly. It was more of a prayer to Bill. Not just a song.

The fitters were the most wicked lot in Hafod Colliery. Walter Molt would wait until all his mates were showered and were lovely and clean, then he would go looking for the dirtiest old trousers or boiler suit he could find and he'd wait for them to dry and go round the shower, soak the suit and then soak the men with it. They were dirtier when they came out than when they went in.

It was Edwin Lloyd who used to look after latrines and the fitters used to play a lot of tricks on Edwin. On this particular day they were in the pit bottom and he had had enough of them taking the mickey, so he waited until they were all in the cabin, then he went for his bucket which was full of chemicals and he made for the hut, stepped in, closed the door and took the lid off. There was no way anyone could get out because Edwin had blocked the only exit. So they had their own back you might say. Edwin didn't mind because he had no sense of smell.

When the baths came first to Hafod. Everybody was going to Gracies, we called it, to buy women's knickers to hide themselves you see. But after about six months everybody threw their knickers away. The Welshman is a shy person because he has lived in a very narrow environment through the years. Some men wouldn't let you go near them. It was funny.

In the baths they would sing everything, just one chorus. It was like a choir. The *Iron Horse* was favourite. And you miss those times. But they are a thing of the past. It doesn't exist among today's miners. It's a pity.

It only needed one to start singing, mostly hymns, and the next thing was the whole baths were singing. You are talking about 500 men now. Whether you had a voice or not it did not matter. The fact is that everybody joined in and it was fantastic.

Before Sunday opening was permitted in Denbighshire some of the younger men went for their weekend drink to a pub near Chirk. The more elderly colliers were concerned that a few of the boys of 15 years or so were also starting to go out drinking.

One morning at the beginning of a shift one of these older men overheard a small wiry lad boasting that he had been to the pub on Sunday.

How much do you drink lad?' he asked with a worried look. 'Two or three pints at least' the boy answered, puffing out his puny chest.

*The Bersham team after completing the roadway to the first 2 Yards Seam.
Emlyn Davies is 4th from the left, back row.*

'Get away with ya' the old man said, now very relieved. 'I spill more than that down my waistcoat.'

Well, this man wasn't a very regular worker and one day he came to work with me. All John was concerned with was his football coupon and those days it was £22,000 if you won the treble chance. So the Under-Manager, Bob Ellis, came in and said one morning:

'How are you getting on with John, has he won the treble chance yet?' then turning to John, knowing he was a regular absentee he asked:

'What would you do if you won?'

'Mr Ellis' the man said, 'I'd have 22,000 days off!'

A team of miners whose task for the day was shoring up the roof with specially made leg uprights and 'H' girders were getting along very nicely when they heard a yell from behind. One of the shift who was renowned for his mutton chop whiskers, had in their haste to get on with the job stood in a position to receive the lowering of the 'H' piece on to the upright. In the dark no one noticed that his moustache had become trapped in the roof and they had left him dangling there like a fly on a fly paper.

One miner well known for his habit of cadging a 'chew' or twist of chewing tobacco received a short sharp messy lesson. Fed up with his request 'got a chew' they mixed mouse droppings and chopped up the tail of a mouse into tiny bits and worked it into a wedge of baccy. Next time he came upon the scene this vile concoction was passed to him. But he didn't seem to notice. When they told him later his scrounging habits were not repeated.

Another miner was very generous with his chewing baccy and offered it freely to all his mates. Unfortunately, he bought a long coil of it and tied it around his waist where it quickly became soaked in sweat. He had very few takers. Maybe he was cleverer than he looks.

The delegate said to the meeting:

'Well boys, the best thing to do now is to decide whether we're going home or down the pit. I know it's a lovely day. What are we going to do?' So Richard Pritchard said: 'I'll throw my cap in the air and if it comes down we'll go down. If it doesn't come down we'll go home'.

He threw his cap in the air and it caught in a tree. Everybody went home!

'There was a fall of ground and just having oil lamps, the lamps went out. Total darkness.

'You all right Bill?' 'I think I am Ned' came a reply.

'Wait a minute then', struggling in the dark they were feeling for each other.

'I'm alright', said the voice. So the other felt his hand over his body.

'Oh no you're not', said the other, 'It's trunked your nose clean off your face ...'

'No!'

Then he realised he had put his hand over his mate's bald head.

An old collier lay dying and news was sent to the chapel. At the mid week meeting the minister stood up and told the congregation:

'Did you know Twm Jack is dying? He has been a member of Zion in his younger days. I think we should go to see him.' So they decided that Mitchell the minister and the senior deacon, Danny Chips, should go to see him. The door was opened by the collier's daughter.

'How's your father?' Mitchell asked. 'Very ill', she replied.

'Can we see him?'

'Yes' she said and showed them upstairs. The old man was lying motionless in the bed. Danny Chips went to the bed: 'How are you?' he asked.

'Pretty bad' the old man croaked. 'Do you realise you're in the river' Danny said. 'Yes, more's the bloody pity' the old man replied.

'Aren't you afraid of the Good Father?' the deacon asked, shocked.

'Afraid of Him' the old man said, 'No' and then he smiled weakly and said

'But I am afraid of the other b . . . . . r'.

An English Underground-Manager took over at Hafod and upset a lot of men by his minute attention to detail and aggresive manner. Knowing he didn't understand Welsh they adopted the practice of speaking Welsh to warn of his approach. Exasperated with his now waning ability to take them by surprise, and knowing they had concocted a Welsh code he eventually went to an Overman and asked:

'What does '*Dyna fo yn dod*' mean?' The Overman told him it means: 'He is here' or 'He is coming'.

'Ah, does it' said the new Manager, and leaping to the new intercom which when a button was pressed gave him a complete open line, he announced in triumph throughout the pit:

'Farrington here *Dyma fo yn dod*' and then he slammed the phone down. But Hafod, being a Welsh pit, the men were not outsmarted for long.

Hafod was famous for its practical jokers. In one case they persuaded a man who couldn't sing a note that he had the best voice in Rhos. This poor man would be coaxed to sing while other miners fixed him with their spotlamps. He revelled in this moment of fame and could also be persuaded to dance on wooden air doors laid on the floor.

He was a real character you know. Where he got his voice from I don't know but it certainly wasn't melodious it was disgusting.

Here is a story which lends credence to the belief that hymn singing and Hafod went naturally together. One Sunday when a maintenance crew were descending in the cage the rope had taken them halfway when because of a compressed air problem it suddenly stopped. After the cage had ceased bouncing up and down the men began to wonder about their predicament. They had no way of telling what had gone wrong or how they were going to get out but it didn't stop them singing. For the next half hour they sang hymns until the cage started moving downwards again to safety.

Swearing in Hafod was almost unheard of, certainly within earshot of those older men who were either chapel deacons or Sunday school teachers, and never anywhere near Bob Ellis.

I can tell you a little story about. swearing now. I hadn't long started down the pit and I went into what was called a heading, that was two men who were proving a new four feet seam and these two men were brothers and I was what they used to call 'tubbing' for them. Taking tubs up to them and to the face. They

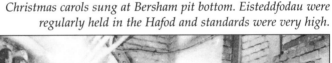

Christmas carols sung at Bersham pit bottom. Eisteddfodau were regularly held in the Hafod and standards were very high.

only had a small face 15 feet by 4 feet and I can't remember whether it was a prop or what, but something hit him on the head and he really had a bad gash, and all he said was 'Oops a daisy' and that was it.

'Tom *Ffyle* (horse in English) now he was a character. There were no helmets down the pit in those days, and Tom used to be on the face opposite to where I worked and we used to use corrugated roof supports which were 7 feet long and about 5 inches wide. They were corrugated to give them a little extra strength, and Tom would never ask a person to help him set one of these roof supports. He would set it by putting it on his head and he had a bald head and now from the beginning to the end of the shift went about with a corrugated head with the weight that he had to use to put this corrugated sheet to the roof.

We had a man working on the Sixes loader, and he was a man who was very Welsh in his speech. We also had a Scottish manager who used to phone the loading point to see how things were going and how many tubs had been filled. The Welshman couldn't understand a word of his dialect. He had a job understanding English anyway so he couldn't catch a word from the Scotsman. So he used to phone Joe Swan, who was the man on the switchboard and say 'Joe, will you take all these messages from this manager and then you can transplant them to me.'

One absent minded collier was always misplacing his 'snappin tin' and accusing others of taking it. After a while this irritated his mates and they got into the habit of nailing his snappin tin to the sleepers so he wouldn't lose it. I don't think he appreciated their help very much.

During the war many men chose to work in the pits in preference to call up. They became known as 'Bevin Boys'. This added a strand of culture that enriched the local community for some of them never went back to their homes. There were a few though who were temporary residents and this story must belong to one of them:

It was explained to this particular Bevin Boy on arrival that he would have to walk at least 3 miles underground to the coal face.

'Bloody Hell' he said, 'No wonder Hitler's declared war, he's found out we're stealing his coal.'

'The foreman was on his rounds and the putter came to him and said:

'The horse is roofin' (that meant that on the horse's shoulders were some nasty cuts and bruises).

So the foreman said to the boy: 'I want you to make this road fit for the horse to travel.'

When the foreman returned this lad had pulled the roof to pieces. The foreman said:

'What do you think you're doing?'

'Well', he said, 'You told me to make the road fit for the horse to go in.'

'Well don't damage the roof' said the foreman, 'Dig under the sleepers and drop the rails.'

So the lad said:

'You must be mad: It's the horse's head that won't go through, not his feet!'

'We had a man who was constantly complaining each and every shift about the contents of his snappin tin.

'Jam again' he would say.

As an electrician he asked me one day if I would go round and do a little job for him which I did. While I was doing this job he disappeared for a few minutes and his wife said to me that he'd gone off to prepare his snappin for tomorrow. So I said to her:

'Who cuts his snappin?' 'He does'.

'Well, who determines what's in the snappin?' 'He does'.

So of course when he emerges again from the kitchen I say to him what will you be having in your snappin tomorrow? 'We'll have to wait and see' he said.

In fact he already knew what he was having and every shift he was complaining that his wife didn't give him this and didn't give him that. The joke lasted for quite a few weeks and he enjoyed it. There was no malice in the pits in those days, no malice at all.

This collier and his wife were sitting by the fireside at 4.30 a.m. and he was getting ready for work. He'd had his breakfast because there was no canteen or any facilities at all. So, as he was going out his wife called:

'John your shoes are on the wrong feet.'

So he turned round, looked at his feet and looked at his wife and said:

'Mary they've been on the wrong feet for 40 years, they should be on yours."

'There were two lads Arthur Roberts and Emlyn Davies working on the haulage in a district called 'Threes'. They were training an innocent young lad called Danny Foulkes. On this day there was something wrong on the coal face so nothing was moving. No coal coming out and the way it came out was through the main gate which was the main road way. So Danny asked his mate Arthur what is wrong. Emlyn said to Arthur:

'We'll have him on. 'Tell him the main gate is locked and they can't find the key.'

Danny believed them. Next thing Emlyn found a long iron rod and he told Danny it was the key for the main gate which the fireman must have dropped when he came in. So they told Danny to take it in to the main gate which is about a mile and a quarter walk. When he got there the fireman asked him:

'What are you doing here?' 'I've fetched the key for you to open the main gate.'

'You soft fool,' said the fireman 'they are making a fool out of you there's no such thing, go back as fast as you can and tell them I'll have something to say when I see them!'

'This lad asked a collier for a chore — that's a piece of bacca. The men who used it thought it would keep their throat nice and moist, anyway this collier would not give him this bit of bacca, so he thought I will get my own back on you. So later he gave the horse a piece of bacca and the horse now with tears coming down his eyes was sick. So the boy had to go out with the horse, and while the boy was going out, the man couldn't fill the tubs with coal and get it away and so he was losing money. As this boy was going out with the horse, you could hear the chains rattling, and coming down the deep to meet him was the Under-Manager.

'The horse is bad Mr Pritchard, I'm taking him back to the stables.'

Now Mr Pritchard's word was law and he lifted his oil lamp up to the horses face and he could see the tears rolling down the horse's cheeks.

'Harry' he said, 'Turn round and take this horse back. He's crying his eyes out because he wants work.'

So Harry didn't get away with his easy day. Mr Pritchard had seen the bacca trick before.'

This miner said to his mate, 'Where were you yesterday, you didn't knock me up. My wife is playing hell about you. We heard you passing so why didn't you knock?'

He admitted he heard him passing but he didn't want to get up out of his bed you see.

The boss was going round one day and there was this old collier sawing chocks. He'd finished his days in the pit, and the old chap was sawing away. Later the manager came out and he was still sawing:

'Is that the same chock?' he asked.

'Well,' the old man said, 'Rome wasn't built in a day.' The Manager said to him:

'I know that, but they did make a start!'

Two miners had retreated into an abandoned heading to stretch their legs and have a rest. Soon afterwards they could hear a noise and realised someone was crawling towards them and when the light appeared they feared the worse. It was the new Under-

Manager and when he caught them he bawled out to them:

'Hey you two, do you know who I am?'

Quick as a flash, the older man turned to his younger companion and said:

'I don't know him, do you Llew?'

The Under-Manager had reached them by now and he said: 'I'm asking you, do you two know who I am?'

Again the older miner outwitted him. Turning to his younger companion he said:

'Hurry up Llew, get on the phone to First Aid and tell them there's a bloke here who's knocked his head and he's forgotten who he is.'

There is a variation in the punchline to this story which is worth retelling. When the Under-Manager repeats his question, the younger man turns to the older and says:

'I don't recognise him, but I think he had onions for his dinner.'

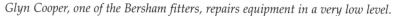

Glyn Cooper, one of the Bersham fitters, repairs equipment in a very low level.

A miner once left his watch very close to where the rock was being shot fired. Too late to get it back he shouted:

'Hell, my watch has been left there.'

When everything had settled after the blast he said to his mates:

'Never mind about the watch, let's try to find the 17 jewels that were in it!'

'This group of miners would pass the chapel graveyard on their way to work from Ponciau and one of them had the habit of saying every morning:

'Oooh you're lucky lying there and we have got to walk all the way to the Hafod, getting up this time in the morning.' So one morning they played a joke on him and one went and hid by the side of the wall of the graveyard and as they were passing the miner came out with his usual remark, and the other man jumped up and shouted:

'You can change places with me if you like.'

Even in the dark you could see his face was as white as a sheet. He didn't expect it you see.'

When automation first came to the Hafod all kinds of names for the new machinery were invented by colliers who could not get their Welsh tongues around the proper name. One old collier on the bus home caused some puzzlement when he kept referring to 'athletic picks'. He was telling the men:

'Ee it's great now. Them athletic picks can get the coal down grand.' The tool he was referring to was an 'automatic pick.'

Some colliers went for a holiday to a farm in mid-Wales and the night after they arrived, they decided to visit the local hostelry. Before they left the old lady at the farm shouted to them:

'I will leave your supper on the hob by the fire.'

Returning much later a little less than sober they looked at the fireside, and one said:

'Oh, she has left some porridge, so we'll have to eat it that's all.'

So they started on it and finished it up. The following morning they got up and the old lady asked:

'What time did you get in last night and did you see a basin on the top there?'

One of the miners said: 'Yes, we seen the basin and we ate the porridge.'

'Porridge' she said, 'That wasn't porridge. I made some paste for papering.'

One of the miners said:

'Oh heck, we won't go to the toilet for years now.'

One childhood memory of a collier now retired is being asked to take out a sick horse by a fireman.

'Ask Dave T'r Oen to give you another one' he said 'but you will have to go down the airway because you can't travel along where the coal was coming in the wagons.'

Everything went well until he stumbled and his light went out. Then coming towards him he saw two bright lights bobbing up and down. Thinking he'd seen a ghost he took to his heels leaving the horse and ran straight into Dave T'r Oen.

'What are you running for lad' he asked. When the boy explained he said:

'It's only the cat. Kept down here to control the mice.'

Recalling some of the stories of her younger brother who was killed at Gresford during the great disaster, I heard this tale:

'Irwin used to lead a pony and one particular horse used to like oranges. Some of the men would take them down with their snappin and throw away the peelings. This pony would smell the peelings and stop. Nothing could make him go until he had been given the peeling. So my brother had to feel around, sometimes on his hands and knees until he found it. Then the pony would walk on again.'

We had horses then and they worked in sixes. Four would go out at a time for a rest. But when they'd gone out the others wouldn't do no work. They'd go on strike. We couldn't shift 'em. They knew they'd been left and would do no work that day.

One miner recalled a time when a party of women were invited to a local pit. By accident or design a large fan was switched on and all their dresses blew above their heads. I imagine that the normal concentration on work was momentarily lost.

'When I got here I found lodgings in Wrexham. In Rhosddu Road it was. There was two of us there and the first morning the landlady said: 'I'll put a savoury duck in your snappin.'

Well, we thought we was alright here. I'd never had duck before. When we opened our snappin there was a piece of faggot. We didn't know then that in Wrexham they call a faggot a savoury duck.

Joe Liner lived in Penycae. He was a character in himself. Rough and ready genial and full of fun. He used to have a habit of being able to drop off to sleep at a minute's notice, and coming from The Hafod on the bus, Darky the conductor that's his nickname would come to Joe who would say, 'Penycae', and by the time his ticket was punched he would be asleep. When we would get to Rhos, we'd all shout 'Penycae', and Joe would jump out in Rhos thinking he was home. But we'd never go without him. We would wait until he got back on to the bus and away we would go.

Then there was another man who was the delegate. When we had a meeting he would use strange long words. He would always use big words and then he would say after he had spoken for about half an hour:

'I will try to make myself clear' and we would all shout: 'Arthur you are clear, as clear as a London Fog.'

A former miner, now the vicar of Gresford, who preached at the commemoration service for the Hafod and other local collieries in Penycae church, used this true story in his sermon:

After he had suffered some injuries underground he was fearful of the blue scar, which is common among miners after such accidents. In the first aid room they asked him:

'Do you want the normal treatment or will you try this new stuff?'

Afraid of spoiling his good looks with the dreaded blue mark, David Griffiths asked:

'Will I get the blue scar?' 'No' they said.

'Right then' David replied, 'I'll have the new stuff.'

The pain was so intense David says he felt as if he had hit the ceiling. But it was worth it. He never got the scar!

I had a phone call one morning from Geoff Williams, the P.R. Officer, I'd just come back from the face and he said: 'Would you go to No. 1, I've got some visitors coming down.'

For goodness sake' I said, 'who the devil's coming down I've just come back from that way.'

'Katherine Hepburn's coming' he said.

'Well you tell her Jackie Coogan will be there to meet her' I said.

Nevertheless I went along to No. 1 pit and who should come out of the carrier but Katherine Hepburn.'

[The reason for the visit was a remake of the film *How Green was my Valley*. All the colliery scenes were shot at Bersham.]

It was another manager by the name of Evans who is believed to have been involved in the following little incident:

One morning there was a knock at the office door and a scruffy young man poked his head in and asked:

'Any jobs going Guv'nor?' Mr Evans called him in and said:

'Look lad, that's no way to go about getting employment. Have you ever tried for a job before?'

'No' replied the lad.

'Well you sit in my chair' said Mr Evans, 'and I'll go outside and show you how it's done.'

The lad now seated at the big desk, Mr Evans went outside and quietly closed the door. After a few moments there was a knock and the lad shouted,

'Come'.

Mr Evans stepped smartly into the room, politely removed his cap, specially put on for the demonstration and began: 'Good morning, sir, would you be kind enough to tell me if you have a vacancy I might fill please.'

Before he could say anything else, the young lad, heaved his legs onto the desktop and replied:

'Not bloomin likely, shove orf' we've got enough of your sort in 'ere already.'

Two miners had come to the end of quite a fierce argument and one finally said to the other, 'you know what you can do, you can go to hell.' A little later one of his mates indicated that he ought not to have said that to the other man, and that he had walked away very hurt.

Sometime afterwards the culprit met his adversary and went up to him and said, 'you know the other day I said you can go to hell. Well I've been thinking about it and you don't have to go!'

Llew Scodyn Evans and Ned Bowker Davies met regularly for the 5 a.m. bus at the Wheelwrights pub in Penycae. This morning an unusual conversation took place.

'What's that under your arm?' said one.

'My snappin', came back the reply.

After a pause the first man said, 'Doesn't look like snappin to me.'

'Of course it is, ya silly b. . . . r, what do you think it is then?'

Another pause. 'Well, it looks like an alarm clock.' Sure enough it was. He had picked up the alarm clock on his way out and left his snappin on the mantelpiece!

A collier and a farmer were talking about dogs. The collier boasted about his prize winning whippet.

'My old boy will beat yours to the rabbit any day' the farmer challenged. So they arranged a match in a local field. The farmer caught a rabbit and brought it in a sack.

'*Dych'n barod?*' the confident collier asked? (Are you ready?)

'Aye, said the farmer and shook the animal out of the sack.

Whippet and rabbit set off at an astonishing speed. But the farmer's collie sat by his side. After a second or two, the farmer murmured, 'Cum ya'.

The collie set off at a wide tangent to the chase and headed straight for the burrows in a small rise. When the rabbit finally arrived he nipped it in the neck and shook it. A second later the panting whippet also arrived. The collier paid his bet.

'Your's may be a better runner, but mine has got a better brain'.

A miner was walking out at the appointed time at Bersham and decided to travel on the coal conveyor, which was forbidden in safety regulations. After a while he noticed a light and quickly got off the belt. It was his overman. 'You were on that belt. That is a two pounds fine for you.' He accused. The miner remonstrated, 'I was not. You couldn't see from there.' 'I saw your light bobbing up and down. You were definitely on the belt' He replied. 'That's not fur' the miner complained. The overman then said, 'All right, I will fine you ten bob (50 pence) and put the money into my favourite charity fund.'

Later that night, in the club, the overman bought the miner a drink. Thanking him for his generosity he said, 'It is kind of you to buy me a drink'

'That's all right son. It comes out of my charity fund.'

Walking out early from a work space was a grave breach of rules. But every miner tried to do it. Supervisors below ground used to prowl around at shift change time to prevent it. An older miner with a younger man tried it and got caught 'You're early' the pit bottom manager shouted.

'No I am not. It is exactly time' and to support his claim, the old miner pulled a large pocket watch from his waistcoat; tapped it and said, 'So there you are. We are on time.'

The manager hesitated. 'Well perhaps my watch is fast. Get on out now.' When he had gone the youngster said, 'I didn't know you had a watch Dai.' The old man pulled it out a second time and winked, 'I don't. It is my baccy tin.'

Point of Ayr colliery from the seaward side. This colliery was the only one in North Wales with all its workings under the sea.

During breaks many miners joined in the underground *eisteddfodau* in the Caban. Smoking was forbidden and most preferred water to clean their throats which became blocked with coal dust. These competitions were often very intellectual and reached a high level of scholarly debate. Often they continued the theological theme of the last sermon in chapel. They could also be light hearted and cause much amusement. A competition for the best limerick brought out this little gem:

> There was a policeman in Llandudno Junction
> Who was completely unable to function.
> But, for years of his life he had been fooling his wife
> By the covert use of his truncheon.

Naturally, they gave him the kitty.

Point of Ayr Colliery was the only pit in North Wales to have all its workings under the sea. For many years it worked 'pillar and stall' methods, with coal faces 12 feet wide. It was always said that the sea bed must be supported. So when the pit had its first long wall coal face which was over 100 yards long, it was with some apprehension that the roof supports were withdrawn to allow the roof to collapse.

One of the miners down there at the time was Will 'Brown Cow'. He was heard to mutter to his nervous mates, 'All right, don't worry boys, but if you see any fish, RUN!'

Chapel, Hearth and Home

There was ten of us altogether, eight children. There was no taps inside. All cold water and bathing in a tin bath in front of the fire. Very dark. Lights on all day and only two bedrooms for eight children. Dad was the only breadwinner then.

There was the old black lead grate and clothes drying on the guard. Everything was done on the fire. Nothing in the house, no toilets. Dad worked ten or twelve hours. Men walked to work in them days and underground too. Some of them districts was a few miles in because they weren't doing mining as they are today; retreat mining, obviously as you are taking the coal out they were going further and further in all the while. They reckoned at one time that Hafod was mining under Marchwiel church.

Clothes were stiff with sweat and had to be hung before the fire in between each shift. It was terrible hard for wives and mothers. This is why a case was made for concessionary coal. You had to be a married man before you could have it. I argued for single men but only married men got it then.

I lived in a row of chamber houses down in Ponciau when I got married and I have recollections of conditions then.

There were four outside taps, no water in the houses at all. The men used to come home black and then the old tub would come out. While they were waiting for the water to boil they used to be sitting on the steps and their wives would shout for them to come when the water was ready.'

The clothes they wore were hard with dried sweat by the time they got home. The old moleskin trousers used to be standing up on their own. Often they sat waiting for water and were too tired to go in for a bath. But they knew there was no way they would get to their beds that night without getting cleaned.

On leaving school at 14 my father gave me instructions on how to impress the manager of Hafod Colliery, Mr John Jones.

'Don't lean against the office wall, keep your hands out of your pockets, take your cap off and call the manager 'Sir'.'

I passed the test and in July 1932 I was given a small piece of paper stamped 'PLEASE GIVE BEARER A LAMP'. This was my passport to my mining life. How proud and important I felt to join my father and brothers in the pit. At home there was always pit clothes around an open coal fire on the fire guard, and stockings hanging from a wire fixed under the mantlepiece. The tin bath and boiler were in constant use. Father made wooden spills to save matches. Bacon fat was kept in a tin and old paint brushes were used to grease our working boots and clogs. Our tin water bottles were hung on a nail in the outside yard with a little water and soda crystals added to keep the inside from rusting.

Miners mothers and wives worked very hard. All cooking, washing, baking and pit washing was done on the fireplace. If a woman was seen out in the street in early morning it was a bad omen, and men would return home. I remember my first job was a powder monkey carrying battery, powder and cable around the district with the fireman. Then I became a haulage hand earning 11s 6d a week.

We'd come back home black. The old bath by the fire and fireguard. Not to stop you falling in the fire but to dry your clothes. Our mothers were nothing more than slaves working. The only time they had extra time in bed was when there was another child coming along. That was typical of every household. But the friendship was marvellous. The conditions we lived in drove people together more than they do today. Because however little you had it was shared.

A jubilant team in Bersham celebrate a new record.
Note the height in which they were working.

It was during the General Strike I remember that Police Sergeant Dan Hughes from Rhos put up a charity cup, and all local teams played for it on the old Cae Dŵr field in Rhos, and that fund was used to buy shoes for the children.

Early morning you could always smell bacon in the village. The miners breakfast then was bacon and an egg, and you have to think of the wives because they were up at 4 a.m. and with men and sons, maybe four or five of them. The problem was hotting water, 'cos they'd all be on different shifts you see. I often think of the wives. She'd have to get the rest of the family off to school. Lunch for the men when they come home. It wasn't only the miners who worked hard. It was the womenfolk as well. But there was something about their character. There was no time of the day when you wouldn't see miners by the Salem Chapel at the bottom of the hill leading up to the Parish Church. They congregated on that corner. Those working nights would come out and have a chat about what they'd done in the pits and share the news. They were very interesting. They would tell you the names of the ponies and if there had been a fall in the pit. And the same in the afternoon.

Charlie Wright and the late John Newton took us in to work then. There were a lot going from Penycae. Two wagons at one time and they were just ordinary canvas top wagons with bench seats. The fare was 4s 6d a week. You had to be at Wrights yard by 5 a.m. for the day shift and they'd bring the night shift home. Then John and Charlie would be on household coal and concessionary coal for the miners families. Then at 1 p.m. they'd take in the afternoon shift and bring the day shift back and then coal deliveries again or haulage work until 9 p.m. Then they would take in the night shift and then went on like that one continual stint. They must have been on their feet from 5 in the morning until after 11 at night.

I remember as a boy my father and most of my family were in mining. There used to be what we called the Mills bus, but it wasn't a bus really it was a lorry with an overhood. They used to sell coal during the day then they would take the miners to the works. For this they would put a tarpaulin sheet thing over the lorry. We would always like to be by the bridge at the bottom of Pentre and he always used to bring with him a butty, just the one, and I would share this butty with my sister. I can't tell you what used to be in it but we always looked forward to it. It was the best thing we ever tasted. I think actually it was because dad's home and he's given us a present. Marvellous.

Crosville laid on a service from Rhos, down Gutter Hill. They would charge you a penny down and one and a half pennies up. Often we worked over so it didn't matter. We walked up the field you know. I've walked those fields umpteen times. When we worked over perhaps it would be two or three in the morning

42

when we finished and we would walk home. Either that or wait until morning for the first bus.

You have to remember that bank holidays years ago were critical times for us. You didn't get paid for Good Fridays or bank holidays whatever. Christmas Day and Boxing Day no pay. You only got paid for the days you worked. So it was a struggle. There were no holidays with pay.

In 1939 we enjoyed our first annual holiday with pay. In the years that followed the build up to the big day affected the whole community. Colliers would count the yards of coal to clear, haulage hands would count the number of tubs to fill. Steps quickened, smiles broadened then the great day dawned for the whole village. It was the Colliers Holiday. Every man would carry home his sack filled with his pit clothes. As we now had pit baths, mothers and wives would welcome their menfolk. Then off with holiday pay to the seaside.

This old neighbour of mine would come home tired at night, have his dinner in his black face and fall asleep on an old mat before the fire, and then get up an have a bath.

I can remember well Mr Frank Evans, Tainant, walking all the way to Hafod. Thirty-one miles must be. I have heard it said that there was a man who walked over the top of the mountain from World's End to the colliery.

Arthur Kynaston, I do remember, walked down from Prospect on Garth Point. Down the fields through Plas Issa, through Hen Blas yard on the way to Wynnstay Colliery. Not even a bicycle.

I can remember as a small lad, men like Mr David Jones, J. R. Hughes and Thomas Hughes walking all the way from Garth to the Coppy Pit in Rhos, which was then by the old railway station. And after a shift, walking all the way back again at night.

Some men you know never saw daylight in winter. It was dark when they started walking from home and dark when they came back up from the pits …

When a man was injured there was no nursing care available at the pit head. Men were taken home on a horse drawn vehicle. The horse being taken from any pit-head job going on at the time.

A man would be there who would patch you up. Then the horse and cart would take you to the hospital. It would be a long time before the wife or mother would get to know what happened. It took a long time to get to Wrexham by horse and cart.

When a miner died no one thought then to clean up the body. It was just delivered to the house. The wife, mother or friends had to clean him. Thank God those days are gone. They had to take him home dead, just as he was. Terrible days. It upsets me when you think of them. But there was comradeship and it was a big asset to be working with such people.

Years ago men bought their own tools when they began work. Many a young lad on reaching his fourteenth birthday has been given his first spoon shovel as a birthday present. Rhos had its own shop selling tools and there was no compensation for miners renewing, sharpening or buying tools to use in the pits.

The centre of education was the Welsh chapel and the week-night meetings. That was where our union leaders had their training in being able to speak and face a congregation or company of men on a public platform. They went to night school after working. There were no day releases. I used to go to the Tech. when I was on afternoons, and the following week I'd go to Wrexham after work. You would have to sacrifice if you wanted to learn in those days.

My grandfather told me that bad language is an uneducated man's crutch, and if ever boys did swear down the pit near me, they would always say they were sorry.

In the Hafod, young boys worked constantly under the eye of older men very often their fathers or brothers or Sunday school teachers. Consequently behaviour was quite strictly maintained. Here a miner recalls being an apprentice in the Hafod:

In them days you had to respect the man you worked for and safety rules came second, but as it is today it's much different. What used to happen if you did wrong or you cheeked anyone down the pit who was older than you, he would automatically clip you round the ear and if the fireman found out he would clip you round the ear, and the next thing you know when you got home was somebody had told your father and he would clip you round the ear, which meant we were more well behaved than anyone. You were not allowed to use bad language down the pit in those days. Because nine times out of ten the fireman would be your Sunday school teacher and it just wasn't on. There was no other answer to it other than a clip round the ear and nobody wants a clip round the ear eight hours a day!

A well known chapel deacon in the Hafod used to conduct prayer meetings before shifts began and whenever there was an accident. Even when he was working in another district. In one incident a man had a finger crushed under a pit prop and after he had been bandaged, the deacon was called to say prayers for his finger.

Religion played an important part in a miners life and the men would go down half an hour early for prayers. It was a great competition for the local chapel choirs. The men would gather in their choir groups at the pit bottom and would sing together as they come up the shaft.

Every man that I knew that has left Rhos village and made his way in life — MPs, ministers, professors, scientists, singers, you name it. It's come from Rhos and their basic foundation; and their learning in the chapel and Sunday schools. I remember going to the Gospel Hall. I remember we used to have over 100 children every Sunday and that Bible reading class was the beginning of education for all these people from Rhos.

In Rhos there was a clogmaker and miners would go there to have boots converted into clogs and for repairs. Inspecting clogs was a regular chore which had to be done and they would either repair their own clogs or take them to Rhos.

As soon as they saw one of the runners becoming loose they used to have their nails handy and it didn't matter what time of the night, the old iron last and the hammer would come out and the runner would be fixed back on, otherwise they would be wearing away the wood of the sole.

Children used to go round looking for old tops of boots because that was all the cobbler needed to make some clogs. The children would go round finding them and the cobbler gave them a copper or two.

As kids we stood outside the shop watching and he used to have a mouthful of these little segs and he would shape the wooden sole and fit the top of the boot over it. Then he would nail it all the way round. This was how the clogs were made in those days in Rhos.

You could always tell when a miner was coming. The steel runner on the clogs made an awful row. You could hear them coming from yards away.

You couldn't waste anything at all. You'd have a pair of work boots, they'd finish ... and you'd take them to the cloggers and they'd cut out a wooden sole on them and turn them into clogs, and you'd have to wear them, like.

Dad was a bit of a fanatic with snooker. He won one or two prizes, and of course was in the Rhos Silver Band. There was a time when there were seven of us in the band and Dad was secretary. If

Anxious families wait on the bank for news of the miner's trapped underground in the Gresford Disaster of 1934.

you like, it was through the Rhos Silver Band that he was killed. He wanted to work on the Friday night and he was in a very bad accident from which he died two days after.

There were no agreed pension rights years ago, men often worked well into their seventies doing light work and this incident is remembered by a Hafod collier:

We were going into this district and I was walking along at the back of the four I was working with and there was an old man. He must have been well into his seventies and his job was in a hollow looking after all the tubs to make sure that the rope was in the centre of the tub. This particular day, the men I was with, namely Bob Hayden, Llyw Flookie, Little Willy and Hywel Roberts decided to stop and they sang a Welsh hymn for this man, because he was fond of singing. You can imagine how touching this thing was. They were singing and the tears were rolling down his cheeks. That's a thing that has lived with me for all these years.

When showers were first introduced in the twenties, men were reluctant to go naked. There was a run on ladies bloomers in Wrexham because the men wore them to take their showers. It also posed a dilemma for fathers and sons and while most of the men went naked and unashamed from the showers, those belonging to the same family would always drape their private parts with a towel. And then there is this story —

Raymond's wife had sort of cultured him to be a gentleman and I remember the baths coming to the Hafod and Raymond was *that* unique that he was the only person who used to wear shorts when he went into the baths, plus the fact that he was the only person who put the canvas sheet round when he had a shower. He would come out dressed in his bath robe and he was made fun of, but he did it throughout the time he worked at the Hafod and he became really respected because he was doing it while we all used to walk about naked as the day we were born.

Lots of miners were afraid to shower their backs. They used to say that water weakened the back. The thought of not being able to earn was so awful that miners left their back rubbing it clean on discarded old sacks, and washed it only at the end of the working week.

The Gresford disaster has its echoes in local people's memories of those who 'might have been there'. Among these stories are the following:

One man whose life was spared was Gwilym Jones of Bradley who was a well known lay preacher in Buckley. He should have gone to work on the Friday night and had to thank an unreliable alarm clock for his life. He worked on Saturday and Sunday with the rescue party.

Another miner arrived for work on that fatal shift but was in such agony with toothache that he was sent home again. While another was walking away from his home when he was swooped upon by a crow. He fended off the bird only to be attacked a second time. Once more he waved his arms about, shooing off the bird. But when the bird flew down a third time he gave up saying, 'Well, that's enough for me, I'm going home'. That night the mine exploded into flames.

A memory of Hafod men never to be forgotten was what became known as the sound of the 'First Rope'. At the end of the shift men would rush to be in the first cage up, hence the 'First Rope'. the cage was a three decker and they would always sing either a hymn, a popular song or the song unique to the Hafod pit, *The Iron Horse*.

All 36 men joined in. The sound at the bottom of the pit was great and slowly diminished as the cage went up to the top. The men waiting to go down would say that the 'first rope' is on its way. It was a sound never to be forgotten and is still talked about by old miners.

Some miners recall being on the first rope and said that it was like stereo

*because if you were on the middle deck you had sound above and below.
Unfortunately a sound nobody was ever able to record.*

It was a tradition at the Hafod that the tally men would not open
the cages until the men had sung a chorus of *The Iron Horse*. More
often than not the tally man and men waiting to go down would
join in the singing as well.

Many miners going to the Wynnstay Colliery would hide their
pipes, twist and matches in the hedge just below Jack Buck's
house, before continuing on their way to work. But the local boys
knowing of this hiding place, would stop off on their way to the
Church School in Penycae, and sampling the twist and the strong
baccy, would continue on their way feeling more than a little dizzy.

There was no Anglican place of worship in Penycae until 1866,
when in January of that year, Sir Watkin Wynn opened the first
National School in the village and this served as a church on
Sundays. Speaking at the opening, the Rev. E. W. Edwards, vicar of
Ruabon, said that the Anglican church had over the preceding
years greatly extended its influence in the district by building
churches in Rhos and Rhosymedre. Raising money for these
projects has meant sacrifices from the working population, most of
whom were men working down the mines, while a few found
work on the land. Sir Watkin who had contributed the lion's share
to the fund was presented with an address by the villagers:

> This populous district has been destitute of those educational
> advances which our more favoured neighbours rightly enjoyed ...
> We are filled with gratitude for the opening of this school in which
> education based upon Christian principles will henceforth be
> within reach of our children'. The Penycae parish church can with
> justification and pride call itself the 'Miners Church'.

With all the pits closing the valley is rapidly going back to nature,
leaving only memories. My funniest moment was opening the

front door very early one morning and coming home black from the pit my husband singing at the top of his voice:

'Why was I born so beautiful.'

Extract from a letter from Caerphilly:

Mining life is one complete circle. You'd end up doing what you did when you first started and as time passed wages would go in a circle with it. So an old chappie ended up on light work; sawing a piece of wood, or opening a door, cleaning or sweeping up and would only have light wages. All his energy and strength had gone to the coal face in the prime of his life. But that was finished with mechanisation, and a man could come off the coalface relatively healthy and strong compared to the conditions that used to exist. Men only worked into their seventies because they knew once they'd finish, they'd starve.

I know what it is to visit my old dad and give him a bit of money at weekends to get a bit of baccy. Each son would do the same and for my mam, for some sweets or something. There was nothing else for them. No pensions or anything. No free coal. That's why they went working. Coal would be brought not in bags but they'd tip it outside the gate. And a retired man would have a wheelbarrow and they'd come to your house and put your coal in. Carry it from the gate to the coalhouse and for all that work he'd get a couple of barrow loads of coal. Then he'd go and do it for somebody else.

The men had to buy all their own tools. If they used powder for exposing, bursting the coal, they had to buy it. There were no safety inspectors at all. All they had was the bare wage for working and slogging all day long. The family depended upon what the man could earn, and that wasn't much. We used to lead a very meagre life waiting for the following Friday.

There is a sense of pride to say that your dad was an old fashioned collier. He used to have photographs taken hanging his tools, and as I have said before, they had to buy their tools. And then they used to patch the old pit clothes until they were threadbare. Then, when we started we would have no work clothes, only handouts passed down. I was very fortunate because I was short and everything fitted me. We never knew what holidays were, nor new clothes and indeed we couldn't sit at the table with out father and mother. They had their meal first. When you came to work that was the time you advanced in life and sat by the table with the grown-ups. We would have, I remember it well, half an egg.

If you wanted a butty, it was bread and butter or jam. There was no bread with butter and jam. It was one or the other. A favourite meal was three penneth of ribs and a stew.

All the bread was home made then. If you went on an errand for a lady, what you would get would be a piece of cake or an apple, and if you were lucky, an orange. It was never money. There was no money anywhere.

A pony was looked after better than the men, because the master would have to buy a pony. I will give you one or two names of ponies I remember. Going back fifty years now there was Budget, Major, Daisy, Moon. We called him that because he was white. Mecca, Collier, Dust, Prince, Bobby, Jasper and Hugo. They knew when danger was coming, and they have saved many an accident by not going forward when there has been danger of a roof fall.

A grieving widow asked her late husband's best mate to collect his ashes from the undertaker. On his way home he called in for a pint at the miners club. Afterwards he took a shortcut through a piece of waste ground and met a friend.

'What is in the box?' he asked.

The miner explained.

'Let's see then.'

The first man opened the box and they gazed solemnly at the dark grey dust. Then the friend tried to put his hand in the box.

52

*Ted McKay (left) and
Islwyn Luke at
Point of Ayr colliery.*

'Show some respect mon,' the miner expostulated and pulled the
box sharply aside, spilling most of the content on to the ground.

'Now look what you have done,' the man shouted in frustration.

'Put it back then, she will never know.'

When this was done and the miner reached the widow's home
she said, 'Not a very big box for such a big man.'

She also opened it and exclaimed.

'How strange. Big man he was, over six feet. Look at him now. A
little pile of ashes and a brown ale top.'

Early on Easter Sunday morning, while it was still dark, Vic
Evans came to the pit and went down with his mate Harry
Ambrose. He would have preferred to be in church in Penycae on
this morning, but there was a job that had to be done.

While they were both walking into the pit, along a level, following them some distance behind was fireman, Wilfred Watkins, another churchman from Johnstown who would also miss the Easter service. Soon he began to sing and his fine voice echoed and re-echoed down the dark and grim underground roads of this hole in the ground, a monument to men's determination and suffering:

> The strife is oe'r, the battle done;
> Now is the victor's triumph won;
> O let the song of praise be sung:
> Alleluia.
>
> Death's mightiest powers have done their worst;
> And Jesus hath his foes dispersed;
> Let shouts of praise and joy outburst:
> Alleluia.
>
> On the third morn he rose again;
> Glorious in majesty to reign;
> O let us swell the joyful strain:
> Alleluia.
>
> Lord, by the stripes which wounded thee;
> From death's dread sting thy servants free;
> That we may live and sing to thee:
> Alleluia.

I can think of no better nor more positive way to end this chapter.

Red Cross — Blue Halo

Accidents can happen suddenly and with great ferocity. This coupled with choking dust and total blackness as lamps are also blown out develops an attitude to incidents and pain that is probably unequalled in any other industry. In this tale a retired miner remembers his own accident and what followed:

In those days you had a borer and he would bore about forty holes and that night the shot firer would come along and he would fire the holes and he would have about forty to fire. The act was he'd fire one at a time. In this particular case there was a band of dirt in the coal and they had to put holes very near together to break it. It happened on a Saturday morning and I'd cleared three yards out of six and in those days if you'd finished your stint you were able to go up, out of the pit, and I was thinking: 'Well I won't be long' — when all of a sudden I put my pick into a piece of coal and I didn't hear nothing only a big flash. My fellow workers heard a loud report but I didn't hear it, my hearing had gone. And I was right on it and heard nothing. What had happened was I struck a live detonator in the coal. This was a dud. It had misfired. Normally they put a guard around it but in this case it was a miscount. But he had 'stemmed' all the holes, all forty, which he shouldn't have done and this one came up in the coal and 1 put my pick in it. I was blown against the belt and I thought it was the finish for me.

I was carried to hospital and was there for three months. I couldn't see but Mrs. Brock (the eye specialist then at Wrexham Maelor) did a wonderful job with me. They couldn't inject because it was my eyes you see and I could feel them scraping and scraping and I heard her say 'Let's save your right eye' and I knew then the left one had gone.'

Hafod was a Welsh pit. The men there spoke Welsh together. If you were English you had to learn it or you didn't know what was going on. But all the safety regulations the miners were supposed to know were printed in English. That's why some accidents happened. Some of the colliers couldn't read English then. Imagine it. But management didn't care in them days. Not as much as they do today.

22 November, 1953 may not mean much to most people but it strikes a chilling cord in the memories of Hafod men. On this night half the workings of No. 2 pit were engulfed in a huge underground fire. Here is a memory of one of the men who fought the blaze:

The fire was fought through a joint effort between the pit rescue teams and the combined fire services of Johnstown and Wrexham. To the non fire service reader it should be explained that while normally the senior fire service officer is in charge of a fire, there are two exceptions. One being a fire aboard ship and the other being underground at a coalmine, where at all times the authority of the colliery manager is paramount. The fire was thought to have been started by a fan motor over-heating, and as it happened on a Saturday afternoon when there was no-one underground it spread along the roadways. It was discovered on Sunday morning when smoke was seen pouring from the up-shaft.

Investigations revealed that it was a serious fire which had spread to over half a mile of the main underground roadway and workings at a point one mile from the pit bottom. The depth of the shaft at No. 2 pit was 1,000 feet. There was a water main throughout the pit but the maximum flow was barely 100 gallons per minute. It was soon realised that this quantity of water was inadequate to control the fire. Mid morning on Sunday at a conference of the Coal Board officials and H.M. Inspector of Mines, it was reluctantly agreed to seal off the affected section of the pit. Workers commenced immediately to assemble the necessary materials, filling sandbags for the sealing operation, which would take another eight hours to complete. In the meantime they carried

Hafod Colliery.

on fighting the fire, and they utilized a 1-inch pipe which normally carried compressed air, used at that time for operating the machinery underground. This pipe was used as a water main and the result was that they were able to use several hoses off this range. At the delivery point the flow of water was 1,000 gallons per minute. The concentration of water began to have results and when the manager saw it he suspended the sealing operation and allowed the fire fighting to continue. By Monday morning the fire was under control and two days later completely extinguished. In this way the pit was saved and was back in production within a week.

Of the two pits, Llay Main never compared with the Hafod. That was due to the airways. The Hafod airways were noted, and that was due to Willie Jones. He had a pen-knife with a hook and you'd find all along the airways and different places his initials 'W. J.' That was to show that he had been through inspecting. That will be there even today. A wonderful mining engineer.

As a boy I can remember the ambulance; and the ambulance man of those days was Steve Donkey from Plas Bennion. They say that he wasn't a very knowledgeable man in many ways, but he was an excellent first aider. I well remember now, you would see him coming up the village with the ambulance and the horse drawing it to Penycae.

There was one terrible accident to Moses Valentine of Tainant. He was caught by the haulage rope and was pulled into the pulley. There was only a thread holding his two legs together, and William Matthews, the ambulance man then, had to take his pen-knife and cut them off. He had to apply tourniquets but Moses never survived. Poor Moses died before they got him out of the pit.

The roof fell in between the girders and smashed my leg up. It was one large piece of rock that fell straight through. It was on the afternoon shift and it happened about 4 o'clock and I was operated on at six o'clock. They had to winch it off me and wheel me out. After that I spent six months in the orthopaedic hospital.

One elderly and sick miner gave me this story of a young boy killed in the fateful night at Gresford in 1934, when 265 miners lost their lives in one of the worst pit accidents in British mining history. Later the mine owners were fined £140 which works out to about 50 pence per life lost.

Any miner in Gresford could have told the management the pit was dangerous. But they were reluctant to complain because they would have lost their jobs. Jokes about the narrowness of the airways were common talk in Penycae and Rhos, but nobody among the management ever bothered to ensure that bad air was escaping out of the pit, properly. Miners would laugh and say to each other, 'them airways are so narrow even the mice run bow-legged'. Another version of the same joke was that mice in Gresford all had 'hunch-backs'. But still nothing was done to improve conditions underground.

This young lad started just a fortnight before the disaster. We had to keep the two doors closed all the while as soon as a journey went through. There would be about eight or ten of them tubs coming through full of coal and he would go down to open the first door and I would be in front and I would open the bottom one so the air could circulate. So that little boy's job was running between the doors when the tubs came.

So that night, the fireman came down and said: 'Are you going to stop on tonight Pete?'

I said: 'No I'm not, I'm coming in in the morning on my usual shift.'

So he said: 'How about you?' to this little lad, he was only about 14 years old and he said: 'Yes, I'll stop on.'

I said to him: 'You're not going to stop on are you?'

'Leave him alone', this fireman said, 'leave him do what he wants.'

'Aye", the lad said, 'I want to see Wrexham play Tranmere tomorrow.'

So anyhow, after the fireman had left I said to him:

'It was Dante's Inferno down there'. Moners prepare for a rescue attempt at Gresford.
[Wrexham Mail]

Bob Ellis, captain of the Hafod
Rescue Team, preparing to re-
enter the Gresford pit in 1935.

'You're a silly lad stopping on instead of going home. I'll tell you what I will do with you, I bet you a packet of Woodbines to a bag of chocolate that Wrexham will lose tomorrow.' [Five Woodbines were about one pence and a bag of chocolate roughly the same in those days.]

Well now the last I heard of him he is down there now. Anyhow you could have a big flame or a small flame on your lamps. Well I was saving my light but this lad's had gone out. So he sent out just before the end of the shift to ask if there was a good lamp and his old lamp came out. I left him mine so the point was my lamp wasn't there neither was my tally. They put me in the paper as missing and not Lloyd until they found out he was down there. He was only a little lad ... he's sitting there now. Poor little lad

I well remember Robert Jones, Trefechan, he was a fireman at Gresford. He used to call at the Cross Keys for his pint, coming down from the Maesydd, and it is known that he said one day: 'We'll all be caught like rats in a trap.' Meaning that the airways weren't good enough. He of course was one that was trapped. There was also a little boy who lived on Pentre Hill, Vincent Matthews. Like other boys he was on afternoon shift and Wrexham Carnival was held on a Wednesday afternoon in them days. Half day closing on Wednesday and they had a wonderful carnival in them days. These boys took the day off to go to the carnival. On the Friday night they had the choice to work an extra shift to make it up, which is what they did. That's how a lot of boys were in that night.

They do say that our late under-manager, Bob Ellis, was one of the leading lights in the Hafod rescue in them days. He hadn't become an official then, he was an ordinary pitman. He was one of the bravest men who went down of any rescue. He was fearless. It was an inferno down there.

The manager ordered a crossing to be done. But it was the wrong way altogether, and one of the men, Little Tim got killed. One of the men still alive was on a kidney machine for a long time. Harry Andrews, it virtually left him crippled. As they were digging him out they were worried about the dets, the detonators, because he was a shot-firer and he still had the dets on him.

Well I remember when I was a girl being told the family tale and being shown a photograph of my great great grandfather John Evans who survived a pit disaster in 1830. My sister and I were brought up with my Nain and Taid in the village of Southsea near Wrexham. My mother had died of T.B. and my father, a merchant seaman on the S.S. *Yorkshire*, was torpedoed and lost his life in the first month of the war, September 1939. Nain would tell us the tale of how her grandfather was buried without food, water or light for 12 days and nights. The story went on to say how colliers went down the pit known as Pentre, Coedpoeth. They were walking in the farthest side of the pit when the water rushed towards them. One man was standing at the highest point and his candle light remained. They managed to crawl 60 yards to an old working, gas getting stronger and they had to extinguish their light. Some men got near enough to a large hole in the roof and shouted to people at the surface who lowered a rope and brought 12 men to safety. By now it was realised that three men were missing, all were family men. It was believed that two men might be alive and that John Evans had drowned. His wife had brought dinner to the pit head at mid-day and had collapsed upon hearing the news. So engines were used to pump out the water for seven days then two men went into the pit. They searched and shouted for days but in vain. Because of the fear of gas no lamps were used and on the ninth day one of the rescuers bumped into one victim and another was found the following day. John Evans body was not found and was believed to be hidden by debris but his wife kept her vigil at the surface and said that she wanted his body for burial. The coffin was made and inscribed 'John Evans, aged 26'. On the thirteenth day of the rescue attempt they came across John Evans' jacket beyond the place where the other bodies were found. They thought they heard a faint 'Hello' but were inclined to doubt it. In

The print of John Evans who was trapped underground for 12 days and 13 nights. Note the two candles bottom right.

a few minutes they heard 'Hello lads', and they found Evans alive, very weak and faint sitting in the dark where he had been for 12 nights and 13 days. My Nain told us how people knelt and prayed by the roadside as he was carried home from the pit. John Evans was able to tell how he managed to make it to above water level and drank drips of water from the roof and ate candles to stay alive. The coffin was taken home and he used it as a cupboard. He never worked again down the pit as miners made a collection which bought him a pony and trap which he and his wife used to take people to market. John Evans lived into his 70s. The colliery owners were so impressed with his survival that they commissioned an oil painting to be done which now hangs at St Fagans, Cardiff.

It is an astonishing story and we have actually got a print of the portrait of John Evans which hangs in the museum and we are very grateful for it.

They would carry injured men on a stretcher. I don't remember even having the opportunity of going to a hospital. They would carry them home and then they would send for a doctor. They would have to come home black as they were, and their mates would carry them. I have seen them coming down the village with a stretcher bringing him home and exactly the same thing would happen if it was fatal and the neighbours would go in and wash and lay the old man out whichever the case might be. There were no ambulances, no safety men and no first aid men.

When Teddy Read's brother was killed they were living in a little cottage in Rhos then. They couldn't get him through the door in the kitchen, he was a big grand fellow. They had to get the stretcher in through the upstairs window and that's the sort of thing that used to happen in those days.

I remember one incident when there was three men working together and they had a roof fall. They were trapped. The men who went to the scene could see them from the waist up. The saddest moment was when we had to run away and leave them. We went back to try and get a covering over them because they were there for many hours. Now we managed to get our hands under their chins. The doctors were there giving them injections and they got them out the following day. One of them died and two were alive. They had to go on dialysis machines because of kidney failure. They were face down and one chappie now if you took the straps off his legs, would fall backwards, but he has been able to conquer it with a stick. He can walk without being strapped up. [See cover photograph.]

When they came to use steel supports the old colliers said: 'We don't like it because we can't hear it cracking.' Meaning that with wood props, they always hear them cracking before the danger point was reached.

There was a lot of accidents with your fingers. You would get burns from your lamp, because the tops were red hot. So we used to carry burns bandages.

My grandmother was a nurse during the Great War and I was left an orphan because my mother died after hearing that my father had been killed just seven days before the Armistice. I remember they used to knock at two in the morning and say: 'We got an accident in the pit.' And there would be an ambulance here. Just a wooden box sort of thing, with a top on and that was the ambulance, and a bit of red cross on it and a horse. They used to take them to Ruabon Cottage Hospital in them days, and when they had to take a leg off, she used to hold the leg while they sawed it off for him. She would hold the leg! She used to tell me that she had never been afraid of death. Afraid of the living, yes, but never of the dead.

It was women in them days that laid out the men in the village. Washing them clean too. They never did for them. I would be well off if I had a penny for everyone I laid out and children too-bless 'em.

By Any Other Name

Some of the nicknames men received were an odd fit indeed. For instance Joe Sloppy was always immaculate when he came to work. There was another family name which was Dirty Dan, but I don't know why. There was nothing dirty about any of them.

A nickname would stick to a man for the rest of his life and beyond. Some gravestones have a man's nickname on them and no matter where you went in the neighbourhood you were known by your pit nickname. Even voting papers for candidates have been printed using nicknames, as well as proper names; also income tax papers, and wedding and burial registers.

Some nicknames have their origins in family behaviour. Like a favourite hat or an attitude to others. Among these can be found Dai Feathers and Dai Swell. Others stem from the Christian name of miners parents, sisters or mothers. Will Nellie, Bill Susan, Jack Lucy and Bill Sophie are an indication of this habit. It would appear that when young boys signed on at the pit, the older miners would ask 'Who's the new lad then', and the answer would come 'You know him, that's Lucy Evans' lad'. The nickname was then fixed — Jack Lucy.

This man always went out with a white scarf. He was known for it. Never went anywhere without this scarf around his neck, and his nickname was Glyn Whitescarf.

When a new under manager arrived at Hafod by the name of Roger Farrington, he was told of the miners custom of finding nicknames. But he wasn't too concerned.

'My name is Farrington', he said, 'they won't be able to do much with that.' But everywhere he went in the pit he left instructions written in chalk and inevitably he got the name of 'Chalky'.

My family had a nickname of 'Mona'. Rumour has it that my grandfather in a small colliery in 1926, General Strike, on Ponciau banks, stole a dog off some gypsies, a greyhound, and he raced it and he used to win money with it and the dog's name was Mona. Ever since then the family nickname went as Mona. He always denied it was pinched. He said he bought it off him, but everybody else told me he did pinch it.

Joe Williams Bugail got his nickname because his family over 100 years ago were shepherds. *Bugail* is Welsh for shepherd. The name has been carried forward in the family for four generations.

Years ago I had a friend. He was the best man at my wedding and his nickname was Dave Dafad. When he was signing the register he looked at me; and my nickname was Joe Bugail, and he said, 'This must be the first time the shepherd has been given away by the sheep!' [*Dafad* is sheep in Welsh.]

A miner arrived to take up a job in the Hafod and lived in Rhos.

'Now you be careful', he was told. 'Anything you say out of place and you'll get a nickname.'

Don't you worry', he replied, 'I'll be like a lamb.'

From that day on he was called Bob Oen. [*Oen* is lamb in Welsh.]

An insurance collector was walking up and down Hall Street, Penycae obviously trying to find an address, and he was being watched by a retired collier. The old man was leaning on his gate with his braces down off his shoulders, contentedly puffing on a knarled old pipe. He watched with some interest until the young man approached him and asked:

'Do you happen to know John Jones. He lives along here somewhere.'

The old man took another puff, stood up and scratched his head:

'No, no I don't think I do. John Jones you say. *Duw*, I've lived here for years but I can't think who that might be.' The young man approaching desperation said, 'He used to be a miner, I think. He's got a nickname, but its a bit rude. Perhaps you might know him. They called him Dan . . . . .'

'Oh!', the old man exclaimed, 'that's me.'

I remember a blacksmith called John Da Iawn, because after every job he said 'da iawn' [well done] and another who was called Johnnie Slater because his father mended roofs. One man who was new to Rhos said he wouldn't get a nickname but because he only had teeth in the front they called him John Central-Eating. It's a well known fact that you don't repeat yourself in Rhos because whatever you said that was your nickname there.

Will Mochyn had a father who kept pigs.
Will Fish because his father was a fishmonger.
Willie Cook because his father was a cook in a canteen.
Will Gwascod [waistcoat] always wore his waistcoat.
Bob Shave because his father was the local barber.

One man came to work in the Hafod saying: 'They won't give me a nickname, I'm too sly for them.' From that day on until the day he died, he was called 'Twm Sly.'

A new recruit at the Hafod was told of the tradition for nicknames. 'I don't mind', was the reply, 'so long as it is something reasonable.' He was called 'Morgan Reasonable.'

One of the Bersham fitters was having a lot of difficulty trying to couple a chain belt conveyer. After a while he started to vocalise his frustration and began talking to himself. 'You'ma won't go, you'ma won't go today', he said as he strained to fix it. Then as an act of exasperation he shouted out to his mates, 'You'ma won't couple today!' Can you guess his nickname? That's right, 'YUMA'.

Johnnie Wooden Leg got his nickname because his father had a leg off after a pit accident. There were no artificial legs in those days. A man would have a peg leg fitted which was similar to a rounded chair leg with a block on the end. The nickname 'Wooden Leg' passed from father to the sons. But it was not malicious and the younger men took to their nickname just like any other. They even used to call themselves the 'wooden legs'.

One miner let it be known that he was afraid of the mice in the Hafod. The infestation of mice down the Hafod pit was widely known. Ever after that, the poor man carried the nickname Llew Llygoden [mouse].

There was a man everyone called Bob Y Gât [The Gate in Welsh] and it was due to the job he had of opening the gates of the cage to let the miners in and out. The same man was also called the Hooker because before electronic signalling the message was sent down the shaft via a big hook attached to wire, and he would pull down on this and a hammer would hit a steel plate on the top of the shaft when everything was alright. Once that signal had been given the winding engine men would set the cage in motion.

We used to call this man Ken the Clock, because he used to go and wind up the Stiwt clock or we called him Ken Pockets because whenever you saw him, he would always have his hands in his pockets.

There was a man from Llay who was nicknamed Ronnie Junkers because during the war he used to watch aircraft going over, and whatever it happened to be, he would say: 'There's a Junker.'

Jack Hughes Floral Dance is an intriguing name until it is explained that it belonged to a miner who had one of the finest baritone voices known in Rhos. He would entertain the miners with his singing, but always gave them a performance of the *Floral Dance*. Other songs he sang to the men underground are *Land of Freedom*, *True to Death* and his favourite hymn, *The Day Thou Gavest Lord, is Ended*.

The boys of the family from Stryt Issa obtained their family nickname of 'Dumpling', from the knowledge in the village that their mother used to make very good dumplings and sell them to make a little extra money. They are still called the 'Dumplings'.

Love spoons are a common item to declare love and proposals. They were once carved by seamen on long voyages. The largest in the world were carved by ex-miner brothers, Ted and Jim McKay using discarded pit props. They are on show at the Greenfield Valley Heritage Centre, Holywell. Each spoon, and its decorative features, was carved from a single piece of wood.

The Sea Lions, and there were quite a lot of them in the family, once kept the public house called the Sea Lion, which was on the corner of Mountain Street and Campbell Street in Rhos.

Some of the roadways and districts in the pits also had nicknames. A famous one was given to a set of steps on a very steep but short new road between No. 1 and No. 2 working. The first person to walk along those steps was Hugh Gaitskell, MP, so they were nicknamed the Gaitskell Steps.

Nicknames given to men in the pits were meant to identify men who may have the same surnames and usually it would work well, but there are cases where those in the family would have completely different nicknames and the origins are obscure.

In another of the Jones Family, one brother was known as Jackie Parry and he had a brother called Albert Bell. Parry and Bell being nicknames with no obvious connection with either men that we can trace.

The family name was Davies and we had three brothers working in Bersham. One was called Ned Socks, the other was Jackie Jane and I can't remember the third except that it was different, and their sister was called Lucy Snot. I imagine the last mentioned was a nickname the owner would willingly have exchanged for almost anything else.

Joe Tattoo got his nickname because he used to have a sideline of doing tattoos. But he got married and so many young boys were going to the house that his wife decided to put a stop to it. But I understand he was really good and quite a few specimens of his handiwork exist in the neighbourhood.

Due to a fall of rock one miner, well known in Rhos, lost part of one of his ears. In the confusion and the darkness the missing piece was not found. Thereafter because he only had 'half an ear', he was known as Dai Six Months.

A NUM official who was always cleaning his nostrils with a forefinger, was nicknamed 'The Picket'.

A miner who said he preferred the long route home was called 'Trunk Road'.

One miner repeatedly used the expression, 'fair play lads' and his nickname became, 'Whistle'.

When the tubs were being loaded prior to being pulled out to the cages, one miner would lift a shovel full, and then pause for a chat. This went on every time and his work rate was well below his colleagues. They complained and he told them, 'I'll fill the last bugger fast enough.' After that he was dubbed 'Final Curtain.'

A miner who had no connection with cows or farming bore the nickname, Will 'Brown Cow' because his grandfather had kept a pub of that name and the nickname was passed down.

Other nicknames of the locality were:

Joe Corwen	Gwyn Fish
Donald Caernarfon	Cyril Jonti
Tommy South	Bill Angel
Lei Denbigh	Rowland Trainer
Vic Mount	Johnny Sealion
Bob Toffee	Bill Sophie
Eddie Swan	Will Saul
Glyn Jack-o-bar	John Jessee
Elwyn Becker	Jim Yantoe
Eric Flue	Wilfred Dwr
Raymond Back	Dilwyn Penwen
Llew Llygoden	Joe Fox & Barrow
Eddie Mona	Jack Queen
Winston Mochyn	Joe Clogs
Emanuel Dirty Dan	Bill Ding a Ling
Albert Fat	Dick yr Hog
Will Cock-a-Hen	Ior Greaser
Less Goch	Norman Sharkey
Ned Socks	Brinley Llewchwith
Ior Margate	Joe Swan
Ned Donkey	Joe Keydie
Eifion Bodoo	Phil Badgers
Twm Sly	Llyw Flookie
John Mangler	Ron Alec
Gordon Garth	Joe Cefn
Idris Talwrn	Alf Scratch
Bill Porthmadog	Willie Dumpling
Danny Swell	George Cigydd
Bobber Cans	George Cefn
Bob Shave	Bob Harlech
John Caernarfon	Brynley Benhook
Will Trawsfynydd	Georgie Cross
Len Penmachno	Gareth Margate
Benny Bala	Eddy Swell
Ior Bullshead	Teddy Delph
John Cabbage	John Dorothy

Twm Dumpling
Dick Fron Heulog
Idris Bragwr
Brian Sealion
Fred Llanarmon
Ernie Criccieth
Jack Toffee
Big Dai
Tommy Shake
Alf Farmer
Will Nelly
Bill Punch
Ronnie Noble
Will Herrings
Donald Snorey
Emlyn Twisty
Brynley Tainant
Eric Flue

Bob Pentre Dwr
Jim Llangollen
John Top
Tommy Coach
Charlie Double
Dai Six Months
Joe Left
Stan Tainant
Bob Gas
John Mandles
Will y Mynydd
Tom Nagshead
Caradog Bobby
Tommy Snoggin
Will Jessie
Jack Nomee
Ike Kiln
Joe Tattoo

Pits and Poets

Lamps and helmets, cans for bread,
　　Round of shoulder, bowed of head,
Cautiously striding, feet of lead,
　　Escaping Nature's Prison,
Here they come …
　　With thoughts of gardens, flowers, sun,
Of children's laughter, ladies love,
　　Bowed in homage to the skies above,
Through all their toil and sweat and pain,
　　In triumph, Christlike, they rise again.

Copyright Mining Industries Christian Association

*Lines on the death of the nine men who fell victims in the
Bersham Colliery explosion, August 1880*

Dear friends you all do surely know
    What happened a little while ago.
What terrible news came to us all
    Of nine poor men whose lives were called.

William Pattison that brave fellow.
    He and his men did go together;
And in the conflict and the strife
    He with his men did lose his life.

Joseph Mathias and Jones as well
    Who in the sad explosion fell.
We hope that in their dying hour
    Were blessed with Jesus' loving power

Thomas Evans and Valentine
    These were two out of the nine.
They were husbands good and kind
    They've left some weeping friends behind.

But they have hope, a glorious hope
    That lifts their sorrowing spirits up;
That when their trials here are past
    They all will meet in Heaven at last.

Edwards, Owens too, and Lloyd have gone.
    No more their face we look upon.
We trust that these and all the rest
    Did lean on Jesus' breast.

Brother Roberts he is safe at rest
    In the bright mansion of the blest.
And he in triumph passed away
    To live with Christ in endless day.

Brother Parry too, a Christian man
    Whose name was on the Wrexham plan.
He always strove to preach his best
    And tried poor sinners to arrest.

Were I to search the country round
    Nine braver men could not be found.
They all did go with one desire and
    Braved the danger and the fire.

All left their home in perfect health
    They little thought of death so nigh;
To call them hence the Lord saw fit
    And to His will they did submit.

Their homes were left in love and peace.
    A prayer no doubt to God was made.
And to perform their task they went
    And down the pit they were quickly sent.

Their families were called to mourn
    That they so suddenly were torn
From their sweet embraces here,
    May God their sorrowing spirits cheer.

They've lost them from the fireside
    Who were their main support in life,
And they do now their loss bemourn
    And here are left to weep and mourn.

© *John Edwards*

The Men of Gresford

Deep down the mine three thousand feet,
    In suffocating dark they died;
Above the air stretched cool and sweet,
    League upon league, to them denied.

No light illumined their dark night,
    No moon, no stars, but scorching breath
of fearful fires in fearsome flight,
    swept them to ravenous death.

O God, whose awful power has hid
    the heat of summer suns in coal,
and men must delve and toil amid
    such dangers and let death take toll.

Look down on them where'er they lie,
    who gave their lives for daily bread,
and let Thine all-pitying eye
    Rest upon us, uncomforted.

And pity us, whose strongest will
    is weak to pay so high a price for warmth,
for livelihood, and still
    stand helpless at the sacrifice!

© *Rhona Roberts, Rhosymedre*

The Miner

Clattering over cobbled stones
　　weary body, aching bones.
Carrying back their soulless dead
　　from that dark and bare pithead.
So grim a burden down the years
　　of toil, and blood and sweaty fears.
Humanity crucified your noble line
　　Eternal '*De Profondus*' is now thine.
From darkness of that well of sighs
　　hourly mute prayers to heaven rise:
'Lord let me see the sun this day
　　Let me hear the children play.
I am so deep and far away'
　　Darkness, black damp, and bloody slime
Fearful fatigue, the clinging grime
　　This damp shroud the brave does fit
They who in toil descend the pit
　　O' toiler sons! So hard, so strong,
Burdened by so many a wrong
　　Wash off the past with bath and towels
Arise to light from Earth's dark bowels
　　mangled men, behold and see
a brighter day doth dawn for thee
　　Men of coal you now have won
a place where cowards shall not sun

ASCEND YE MINERS
AFC

Contributed by NUM Wrexham

The Iron Horse

This song is unique to the Hafod Colliery. It is thought to be the composition of Bill Thomas, the Head Fitter. The Iron Horse *was sung regularly and with great affection on the 'first rope' and in the baths after a shift. But most significantly it became the song of the fitters who believed that when all else failed and a piece of machinery refused to function it would burst back into life when the fitters had sung the* Iron Horse. *Oddly enough legend has it that it quite often proved to be a remedy that worked!*

I has some little chickens
    A large chicken run.
But owing to conditions I'm now down to one.
    I feed him all the tit-bits, the poor
little thing,
    and just to keep him up to scratch
I go to him and sing:

Hoorah for the Iron Horse
    He travels along his course
His food is fire, he never can tire
    this marvellous Iron Horse.

Over rivers we see him fly and over the
    mountains high
A mile he'll go in a minute or so,
    This marvellous Iron Horse.

Cerddi a Baledi
[Poems and Ballads]

I. D. Hooson

Y Lamp

Wedi Tanchwa Gresford, Medi 1934

Fe ddeil y lamp ynghyn
    Ar fwrdd y gegin lom,
A'i fflam fel gobaith gwyn
    Drwy oriau'r hirnos drom.

Mae'r drws o led y pen,
    Er oered gwynt y nos;
Pwy ŵyr na ddaw y llanc
    Yn ôl cyn hir i'r Rhos?

'Mae'n gorwedd,' meddai rhai,
    O dan y talcen glo,
A'r fflam yn fur o dân
    O gylch ei wely o.'

Ond, yn y bwthyn llwyd
    Mae un o hyd a fynn
Ddisgwyl ar drothwy'r drws,
    A chadw'r lamp ynghyn.

Yr Eos

Ni wn pwy daenai'r stori
    Fod eos rhwng y drain,
Yn canu'i chalon allan
    Ym mherthi Bryn-y-brain;
Ond cerddem yn finteioedd
    Dan olau'r lleuad fain,
I wrando cân yr eos
    Ym mherthi Bryn-y-brain.

Ni wn a glywodd undyn
    O'r dyrfa honno 'rioed
Y mwyn aderyn cefnllwyd
    Yn canu yn y coed;
Ond gwn mor llon y teithiem
    Ar draws y caeau glas,
A'r hyfryd ddisgwyl wedyn
    Dan gysgod coed y plas.

I dawel lys yr hafnos
    Ni ddaeth y cantor pêr,
Ond melys oedd yr aros
    A'r disgwyl dan y sêr;
Disgwyl y gerdd nis canwyd,
    Gwrando y gân ddi-lef —
A gobaith yn creu nefoedd
    O'r addawedig nef.

Mynwent Bethel

Mae'r 'Bedol' ar yr aswy
    A 'Bethel' ar y dde,
A'r fynwent yn y canol —
    Hir gartre' plant y dre;
Daw holl ffyddloniaid Bethel
    A'r Bedol yn eu tro
Yno i gadw noswyl
    A chysgu yn ei gro.

Mae Huws, Y Grosar, yno —
    Y blaenor wyneb trist,
Ei ddagrau wedi'u sychu
    Am byth o fewn y gist;
A Wil, y Glöwr rhadlon,
    A feddwai ambell dro —
Mae yntau'n gorwedd yno,
    Heb syched, yn y gro.

Fe garai Wil y meysydd
    A'r llwyni drwy ei oes,
Cwningen a 'sgyfarnog
    A milgi hir ei goes;
Mewn cân a chwmni diddan
    Y treuliai lawer awr,
Dan gronglwyd glyd y Bedol
    Ar fainc y gegin fawr.

Ond gwynfyd Huws, y Grosar,
    Oedd gwrando'r bregeth hir;
Ni welodd Huws ryfeddod
    Mewn maes na choedlan ir;
Rhwng meinciau Capel Bethel
    A chowntar Siop y Groes
Y cafodd ei ddiddanwch
    A'i nefoedd drwy ei oes.

Bu'r ddau yn dadlau'n fynych
    Dros hawliau'r chwith a'r dde —
Ond heddiw maent yn dawel
    Ym mynwent oer y dre;
Yn aros awr y ddedfryd
    Rhwng muriau'r carchar llaith
Y tystion wedi'u galw,
    A'r rheithwyr wrth eu gwaith.

Pwy ŵyr beth fydd y ddedfryd
    A rydd y rheithwyr call;
'R oedd beiau a rhinweddau
    Yn eiddo'r naill a'r llall;
Ond weithian, mwyn fo'u cyntun
    Ym mynwent drist y dre,
Y Bedol ar yr aswy,
    A Bethel ar y dde.

Gwin a Cherddi Eraill
[Wine and other poems]
I. D. Hooson

Yr Hen Lolfa

Ger muriau Parc Syr Watcyn,
    Ar fin y briffordd lefn
Sy'n arwain tua'r Berwyn
    Drwy'r Green a phentre'r Cefn,
Bu dynion wrthi'n brysur
    Yn cloddio'r pyllau glo,
A'r mwg a'r llwch yn cuddio
    Glesni a thegwch bro.

Chwyrriellai yr olwynion,
    A chlywid rhonc a rhoch
Gwagenni a pheiriannau,
    A gwlch hwteri croch;
Ac ar y llain adwythig,
    Yn garnedd hagar, ddu,
Ymwthiai'r domen rwbel
    Ei phen i'r nef yn hy.

Ond llonydd yw pob olwyn
    A pheiriant erbyn hyn,
A than y rhwd a'r mwswg
    Maent heddiw'n cysgu'n dynn.

Ni chlywir rhu na hisian
 Na gwich un hwter groch,
Ac yn hen Barc Syr Watcyn
 Y pawr yr elain goch.

Fe ddaeth rhyw arddwr heibio
 I wisgo'r domen brudd
A rhoncwellt tal, a rhedyn,
 A blodau pinc eu grudd.
A heddiw clywais fronfraith
 O ardd y pyllau glo,
Yn moli'r Garddwr hwnnw
 Am adfer tegwch bro.

Y Brain

'R oedd miri bore heddiw
    Ym mrigau coed y plas,
A chlywais wrth fynd heibio
    Y brain â'u lleisiau cras
Yn gaiw ar ei gilydd,
    A rhai yn dadlau'n gas.

A choflais am y fintai
    A ddeuai ar ei hynt
I'n pentre' ddechrau gwanwyn,
    I ffeiriau'r dyddiau gynt,
A'i thwrw mawr yn gymysg
    A sŵn y glaw a'r gwynt.

A gwyddwn fore heddiw
    Wrth wrando yn y glaw
Ar sŵn y fintai gyntaf
    A glebrai mor ddi-daw
Fod mintai fawr y Gwanwyn
    A'i charafan gerllaw.